the facts about
LIGHT

Rebecca Hunter

FRANKLIN WATTS

First published in 2003 by
Franklin Watts
338 Euston Road
London
NW1 3BH

Copyright © Franklin Watts 2003

Franklin Watts Australia
Hachette Children's Books
Level 17/207 Kent Street
Sydney NSW 2000

ISBN: 978 0 7496 7275 1

A CIP catalogue record for this book is available from
the British Library

Printed in China
Planning and production by Discovery Books Limited
Editor: Rebecca Hunter
Design: Keith Williams
Consultant: Jeremy Bloomfield
Illustrations: Keith Williams: page 8, page 18, page 23;
Stefan Chabluk: page 19

Photographs:
Bruce Coleman Collection: Cover (Pacific Stock), page 4
(Gerald S Cubitt); Corbis: page 7 top, 14, 17, 19, 29;
Discovery Picture Library: page 12 top, 20 top, 22;
NASA: page 8; Oxford Scientific Films: page 4 (Konrad
Wothe), 5 (John McCammon), 7 bottom (Satoshi
Kuribayashi), 9 (Michael Leach), 10 (John Gerlach), 12
bottom (Michael Leach), 15 (Alastair Shay), 16 (Colin
Monteath), 20 bottom (David M Dennis), 21 (William Gray),
23 (Konrad Wothe), 25 (Adam Jones), 26 left (Michael
Fogden), 26 right (Belinda Wright), 28 left (Richard Kolar);
Photodisc: page 6, 24; Science Photo Library: page 11
(Keith Kent), 13 (Dr Fred Espenak), 27 (Pascal Goetgheluck),
28 right (Will & Deni McIntyre).

Franklin Watts is a division of Hachette Children's Books.

the facts about

LIGHT

Contents

Words in **bold** appear in the glossary on page 30.

What is light?

Without light, life on Earth would be impossible. Sunlight provides the **energy** that keeps all living things alive.

Light is a form of energy, like heat and sound. Heat is energy that we can feel, sound is energy that we can hear, light is energy that we can see. We mostly see things because light bounces off them into our eyes. Nearly everything in our world bounces, or **reflects**, light and this is how we see.

▼ Very bright light can seriously damage your eyesight. This is why you should never look directly at the Sun, even through sunglasses.

You can do it...

Try living without light! Blindfold yourself for an hour to see what life is like without light. Try to eat a meal with your blindfold on. You will need someone to help and make sure you don't hurt yourself.

The energy from the Sun powers all life on Earth. Without it the planet would become dark and cold and all living things would die.

▲ Sunlight is not just something to be enjoyed at the beach – it is essential to all living things.

All green plants need light to survive. They use the energy in sunlight to make sugars that help them grow. Plants are the first step in the food chain that provides food for animals and, eventually, humans too. Most animals need some light so that they can see to find food and shelter. They also need to be able to see in order to get away from **predators** that might eat them. People need light to be able to read and to write, to work and to play. Living without light is difficult even for a short time. Imagine what the world would be like if there was no light at all.

key facts

- Light is a form of energy that we can see.
- All living things depend on light.
- We see most things because they reflect light.

Sources of light

All light comes from a **source**. Some light sources are natural, some are **artificial**.

The Sun

By far the largest source of natural light on Earth is the Sun. The Sun is a star, an enormous ball of glowing gases that gives off vast amounts of energy in the form of heat and light. The temperature on the surface of the Sun is 5,500°C (10,000°F).

Other stars

The other stars are also sources of natural light. There are billions of stars in our **galaxy**. They look small because they are very, very far away from us. If you look up at the sky on a clear night, you will see about 3,000 stars, each one of which provides us with a tiny amount of light.

Artificial sources of light

Artificial light is usually made by people. Firelight, candlelight, gaslight and electric light are all forms of artificial light. Like the Sun and the stars, these artificial sources produce heat as well as light. But not all forms of light are hot.

▼ The Sun is Earth's greatest source of light.

▲ Halloween lanterns provide artificial light.

Cool lights

Fluorescent lights that brighten streets, shops and offices are made by passing an **electric current** through a glass tube filled with a gas. This makes the gas glow, but the light is cool, not hot. Different gases produce different-coloured light. Neon gas always gives out a red light. Argon gas produces a white light. **Chemical reactions** can also produce cool light. Some animals, like fireflies, can make light within their bodies in this way.

Reflectors

Some things appear to be sources of light, but are actually reflecting it. The Moon seems to shine brightly at night, but it is in fact just reflecting the Sun's light.

▼ Fireflies are not flies, but night-flying beetles. Light-producing chemicals in their bodies enable them to signal to each other.

key facts

- ○ All light comes from a source.
- ○ Sources can be natural or artificial.
- ○ The Sun is the biggest source of light on Earth.

Night and day

At any one time, half the Earth is in sunlight, while the other half is in darkness. Because the Earth is always turning, this gives us day and night.

The Sun can only shine on one half of the Earth at a time. There it is daytime. The other side of the Earth faces away from the Sun and there it will be night-time. As the Earth turns, the areas in sunlight will move into darkness.

Being active at night

In the days before electric light was invented, most people had to stop work when it got dark, and go to bed. Now we can carry on our lives under artificial electric light. Many people such as doctors and nurses, police officers, fire-fighters, factory workers and paramedics have to work through the night.

▲ This picture taken from space shows how half of the Earth is in sunlight while the other half is in darkness.

▼ When it's daytime where you are, it will be night-time on the other side of the world.

Sun

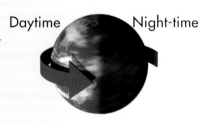

Daytime   Night-time

Earth

Nocturnal animals

Many animals only come out at night. They are called nocturnal animals and have **adapted** so they can move about in the dark. Owls have large eyes that can see very well in dim light. Bats have an amazing sense of hearing. The high-pitched squeaking sounds they make bounce off objects, helping them to locate **prey** such as flying insects.

key facts

- Half of the Earth is in sunlight, and half is in darkness.

- The Earth turning is what makes daytime and night-time.

- Nocturnal animals are active at night.

Properties of light

Light has three important **properties**. It travels in straight lines. It travels very fast. It cannot travel through most things and therefore makes shadows.

Light rays

You can see how light travels in straight lines when sunlight is streaming through a window. The light shines on tiny pieces of dust in the air and you can see the lines of light.

When you are in a car in the dark, the headlights light up the things in front of you, but the light rays cannot shine on things around the corner.

You can do it...

Turn on a torch at night and see the straight light rays. You might be able to see them more clearly if you sprinkle some talcum powder into the beam of light.

Speed of light

Light travels very fast. The speed of light is the fastest speed known; nothing can travel faster. The actual speed of light is 300,000 kilometres (186,000 miles) per second. This is very much faster than the speed of sound, which is 340 metres (1,130ft) per second. You can see this difference in speed during a thunderstorm, when you see the lightning (light) before you hear the thunder (sound).

◄ The Sun's rays can be seen clearly shining through the morning mist.

Calculate how far away a thunderstorm is. When you see a flash of lightning, start counting slowly. Stop when you hear the thunder. For every count of three, the storm is about one kilometre away (a count of five is equal to about one mile).

Blocking light

Most objects in the world are **opaque**. This means light cannot pass through them. Because light rays cannot bend around things, a shadow is formed on the other side of the object. The Earth is an opaque object. When the Sun shines on one side of it, the other side is left in shadow.

key facts

- Light travels in straight lines.
- Light travels very fast.
- Opaque objects block light and form shadows.

Shadows

Shadows are formed when light hits an opaque object. The light cannot shine through it and a shadow is made.

Outside and during the day, most shadows are formed by the Sun. When you stand with your back to the Sun, you can see your shadow on the ground in front of you. The length of your shadow depends on where the Sun is in the sky. During the early morning and late afternoon, the Sun is low in the sky and you will have a long shadow. At midday, when the Sun is directly overhead, your shadow will be short.

Sundials

A sundial is a clock that uses shadows to tell the time. As the Sun moves across the sky, the shadow made by the sundial moves around and points to numbers showing the hour.

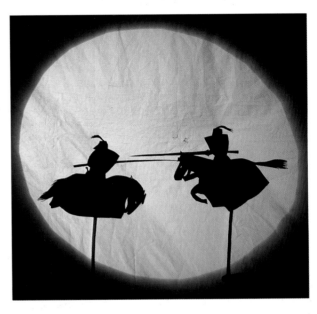

▲ In some countries people use shadows to create puppet shows. Many traditional stories are told through these shadow plays.

You can do it...

Make your own sundial. Push a long, straight stick into the ground. At each hour during the day, mark the position of the Sun's shadow with a smaller stick. You can then add labels to the small sticks to show the time.

Eclipses

The most spectacular shadows of all are those cast by the Earth and the Moon on each other when they block the light from the Sun. During an eclipse of the Sun, the Moon passes between the Sun and the Earth, casting its shadow on the Earth's surface. If you are in exactly the right place, the Sun is hidden from view and it becomes night for a few minutes, until the Moon moves on. During a lunar eclipse (below), the Earth passes between the Sun and the Moon. The Earth's shadow moves across the Moon, slowly covering it with darkness.

▼ During a lunar eclipse the Moon does not disappear completely. Some light is reflected from the Earth, making the Moon appear red.

key facts

- Outdoors, the length of a shadow depends on the position of the Sun.

- A sundial uses a shadow cast by the Sun to tell the time.

- During an eclipse the Earth or Moon block the Sun's light for a short time.

Letting light through

Light can pass through some materials. These materials are either transparent or translucent.

Transparent materials

If you put an opaque object in the path of a beam of light, it will block the light and make a shadow. If an object is transparent, nearly all the light will pass through it.

The most transparent substances are pure air, pure water and pure glass.

▼ Clear water is almost transparent. That is why you can see these divers so clearly under the water.

Translucent materials

Many objects are translucent, which means they let some light shine through them. For example, clouds are translucent and allow some of the Sun's light to pass through them; if they were opaque, it would be as dark as night on cloudy days.

Other translucent materials include fabrics, paper, ice, some plastics and coloured glass – as used in stained-glass windows, for example. Translucent materials make useful sunshields. They cut out the glare of bright sunlight, but you can still see through them. Sunglasses, blinds and frosted glass are all made of translucent materials.

You can do it...

Make a stained-glass window. Draw a picture in black pen on a piece of tracing paper. Colour the picture carefully with felt pens. Stick the picture on to a window. It will look spectacular when the Sun shines through.

Reflected light

When light hits an object it bounces off it in all directions. This is called **reflection**.

Some objects reflect light better than others. How well an object reflects light depends on its surface. Smooth, light-coloured objects reflect light better than dark, rough objects. Some things reflect light so well that they almost appear to give off their own light. Still water, shiny metals, mirrors and the Moon are all good reflectors of light.

▼ Lake Tekapo in New Zealand. The still water reflects the light beautifully.

Mirrors

Mirrors reflect so much light that they make an almost perfect reflection. The reflection that a mirror makes is called a mirror-image. However, a mirror-image is not exactly the same as the original. The right side of the original appears on the left side of the mirror-image.

You can do it...

Try writing in 'mirror writing' that can only be read in a mirror. Some letters have a strange effect in the mirror. Write 'CODE BOOK' and then turn the paper upside down and look at it in the mirror. What other letters will have this effect?

Mirrors are used in many ways. Most of us look into a mirror every day to see how we look. Before glass mirrors were invented, the Greeks and Romans made mirrors out of polished bronze. Dentists use small mirrors to see inside their patients' mouths. Mirrors are used in cars so we can see other traffic behind us.

key facts

- All objects reflect light.
- Mirrors make an almost perfect reflection.
- A reflection in a mirror is called a mirror-image.

Seeing

We see things when light from a source enters our eyes. This can happen in two ways.

Light may come directly from the source to your eyes, as happens when you look at an electric light bulb or the flame of a candle. Light is also reflected off objects and into your eyes. This is how you see all objects that are not light sources.

◀ A candle is a source of light. The light shines directly into our eyes. This is how we see it.

Eyes

Light enters the eye through a hole called the pupil. It then passes through the **lens** which bends the light and focuses it on to the retina. The retina is the part of the eye that allows us to see in colour. The retina sends a message to the brain, and the brain tells us what we are seeing.

▼ The human eye. Light rays reflected off an object enter the eye through the pupil. The lens focuses these light rays on to the retina, where the image appears upside down. The brain turns the image back so we see it the right way up.

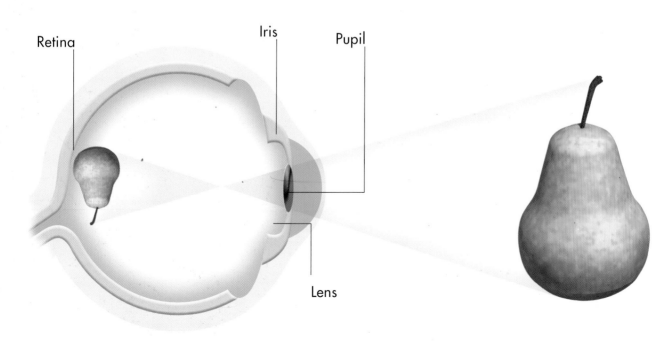

Retina

Iris

Pupil

Lens

▶ The pupil controls how much light is let into the eye. When the light is bright, the iris contracts and the pupil closes to a small hole that only allows a small amount of light to enter. When the light is dim, the pupil opens wide to let in as much light as possible.

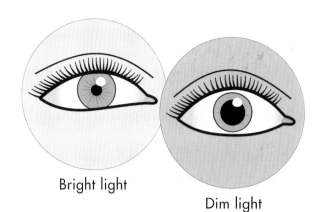

Bright light

Dim light

Lenses

Lenses bend light rays. Anything with a clear, curved surface can act as a lens. When you look through a lens it can either make things seem closer and larger or further away and smaller. People whose sight is not very good often need to wear lenses so they can see better. Contact lenses are worn on the surface of the eye. Glasses are a pair of lenses in a frame.

You can do it...

Try making a lens. Fill a small, empty jam jar with water and screw on the lid. Roll the jar slowly over the writing in a book or a newspaper. What do you notice?

key facts

⬭ We see most things because light is reflected off them into our eyes.

⬭ Lenses can bend light rays.

⬭ People wear lenses to help them see better.

White light

The light from the Sun is called '**white light**'.
White light is actually make up of many colours.

A triangular piece of glass called a prism can separate the colours out of white light. When light goes through a prism, it is slowed down and bent. It separates into colours that spread out when they leave the prism.

Colours always come out of a prism in the same order, with violet at one end and red at the other. This is called the **spectrum** of light.

Look at the underside of a CD (left) in the light. If you twist and tilt it, you will be able to see the whole spectrum of colours.

▼ A beam of light shining through a prism will show all the colours in white light.

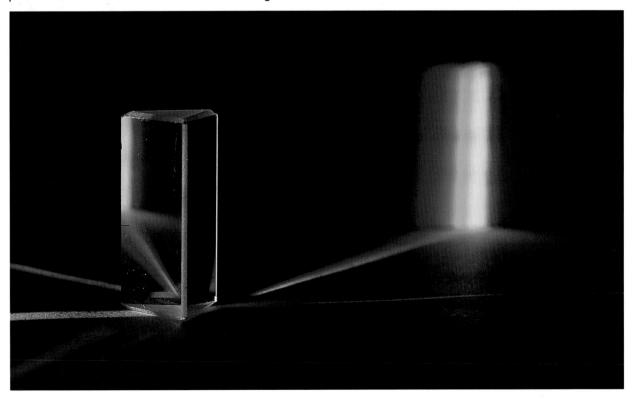

Rainbows

Perhaps the most spectacular example of the spectrum is a rainbow. A rainbow occurs when sunlight falls on raindrops. Each raindrop acts like a tiny prism and splits the light up into the so-called 'colours of the rainbow'.

▼ A rainbow has all the colours of the spectrum: red, orange, yellow, green, blue and violet.

You can do it...

Make your own rainbow. Turn on a hose and adjust it so it makes a very fine spray. Stand with your back to the Sun and spray the water into the air. You should be able to see your very own rainbow.

key facts

- White light is made up of many colours.

- A prism can separate light into colours.

- The range of colours in white light is called the spectrum.

Colours and pigments

Coloured objects absorb all the colours in white light – except the colour they are, which they reflect. This is the colour we see.

White objects reflect all the colours of light. Because all the colours are being reflected, the objects appear white. A carrot absorbs all colours except orange. Orange light is reflected and we see the carrot as orange. In contrast to white, which reflects all colours, black objects absorb all colours so we see nothing but black.

Blue skies

Light is scattered, or bounced around, by almost everything it hits, including air. Air scatters blue light but not the other colours in the Sun's rays. This is why the sky looks blue to us. The Moon has no air to scatter light and so the sky on the Moon appears black.

Pigments

Pigments are chemicals that absorb the light of some colours and reflect other colours. Pigments are used in paints to colour things. They can be made from plant or animal material, ground-up rocks or chemicals.

▼ A selection of fresh vegetables shows just how many bright colours there are in nature.

Mixing paints

In painting there are three primary colours: blue, red and yellow. These can be mixed together to make almost any colour except white. If you mix the three primary colours together you get black.

Mixing light ▼

Mixing light

Mixing the colours of light is different to mixing paint colours. In light there are three primary colours: red, green and blue. You can mix these colours in different proportions to give any colour in the spectrum.

Mixing paint ▼

▼ When the Sun is close to the horizon, it has to shine through a thicker layer of air than when it is high in the sky. This air is full of dust, smoke and drops of water which scatter light in a different way. This makes the Sun and sky look red or orange at sunrise and sunset.

key facts

- The sky is blue because air scatters blue light.
- Pigments are used to colour paint.
- Colours can be mixed to make other colours.

Plants and light

Light is very important to plants. They make food from sunlight in a process called **photosynthesis**.

Life on Earth could not exist without plants. Plants provide animals with food to eat and **oxygen** to breathe. We need plants and plants need light.

Photosynthesis

Plants use sunlight in order to grow. They do this by a process called photosynthesis. Using a green substance called chlorophyll in their leaves, the plants capture the energy in sunlight. Together with water from the soil and the gas carbon dioxide from the air, this energy is changed by chemical reaction into sugars. These provide the plants with energy for growth. As part of this process, the plants give off the gas oxygen.

You can do it...

See how plants need light. Cut a shape out of a piece of thick paper – the initial letter of your name is a good shape to use. Fasten this with sticky tape to the top side of a big leaf. Leave it for two weeks and then remove it. The letter will show up yellow on the leaf where the paper has blocked out the light.

Plant growth

From the moment a seedling grows out of the dark soil, it seeks sunlight. As a plant grows bigger, it continues to grow towards the source of light. It is important that each leaf receives as much light as possible, so a plant will adjust its leaves during the day to follow the position of the Sun.

In a thick tropical rainforest, plants compete with each other for light. Trees grow very tall to try and reach above the others. Low-growing plants have to survive in very dim conditions. They grow extremely large leaves to catch as much of the available light as possible.

▲ Sunflowers turn to follow the Sun as it moves across the sky.

key facts

- Plants depend on light to grow.

- Plants capture the energy in sunlight by photosynthesis.

- Plants compete with each other for light.

Animals and light

Animals do not depend on light in the same way as plants, but they still use light in many ways.

Using colours

If you look around the animal world you will see the range and depth of colours they use. However animal colours are not there to impress us: they all have a purpose.

Many animals use colours to disguise themselves so that they are not visible to predators. This is called camouflage. A butterfly may look like a flower, or a fish like a stone. As its name suggests, a dead-leaf mantis looks just like a dead leaf and is almost invisible to its enemies.

▼ Some bower birds are attracted by the colour blue, and collect whatever blue things they can find to add to their bower.

▲ The tiger is camouflaged by its stripes, which match the dark and light patterns of the long grass in which it lives.

Attracting a mate

Some animals use colour to attract a mate. The male peacock shows off to females with the amazing display of his colourful tail. Bower birds also engage in colourful courtship displays, but instead of using their own feathers they put together a strange collection of berries, shells, flower petals and even bits of shiny glass or metal. With this they hope to attract a female to their 'bower'.

Warning colours

Colour can also be a warning to other animals. The black and yellow stripes of a wasp are unforgettable. Once you have been stung, you will keep away from wasps in the future. Hoverflies have adopted the wasp's stripes. Although they are harmless, predators think they will sting like wasps so they leave them alone.

Living without light

The bottom of the sea is one of the darkest places on Earth. It is too dark for plants to survive but some animals do manage to live there. Some of these make their own light by a process called bioluminescence, using light organs dotted around their bodies.

These animals use bioluminescence in different ways. The flashlight fish uses flashes of light to signal to other flashlight fish and for hunting. Some fish, such as the anglerfish, use their light organs like fishing rods and lure their prey close by to be eaten.

key facts

- Animals use colours to disguise themselves, as a warning and to attract a mate.

- Some animals can make their own light; this is called bioluminescence.

▶ A jellyfish glows with bioluminescence after being disturbed by a passing ship.

Using light

We switch on electric lights every day of our lives and think little of it, but light is being used all the time in many other interesting ways.

Cameras

Cameras work a bit like our eyes. A beam of light passes through a lens. This directs the image on to the film where it is then fixed. Later the picture can be printed out on special paper.

▼ One of the most spectacular examples of light in action is a firework display. The lights are produced by exploding gunpowder.

Fibre optics

Fibre optics use fine, flexible cables with insides that are very reflective. Light travels along these cables, bouncing from one side to the other – even around corners. No light is lost from the side of the cable, so a light shone in at one end comes out, just the same, at the other.

Fibre optics are useful for seeing into awkward places. Doctors use them to see inside a patient's body. They also link up **telecommunication** systems all over the world.

Lasers

A laser produces a thin beam of light that is the brightest light known. Laser light is so strong it can burn a hole through steel.

Lasers have many uses. In industry they cut through thick steel sheets easily and precisely. Surgeons use laser beams to do delicate operations on the eye and to attack cancer cells.

Because laser beams travel in such a straight line, they are valuable as tools for **surveying**. A laser was used to plot the course of the Channel Tunnel under the sea.

key facts

- Cameras use light to capture images on paper.

- Fibre optics are cables that can carry light around corners.

- A laser is a device that sends out an intense beam of light.

Glossary

Adapt The way in which animals and plants change over many generations to survive better in their particular environment.

Artificial Made by humans rather than occurring naturally.

Chemical reactions A reaction that takes place between two or more substances in which new substances are produced.

Electric current The way that electricity flows through a wire or cable.

Energy The power that makes things move, light up, make a sound or get hotter.

Focus To adjust so that the image is clear.

Galaxy An enormous group of stars.

Lens Something that can change the direction of a beam of light.

Opaque Something that does not let light pass through it.

Oxygen A gas in the atmosphere.

Photosynthesis The method by which plants make food from sunlight, water and carbon dioxide.

Predators Animals which live by eating other animals.

Prey Animals that are hunted by other animals.

Properties In science, the qualities that a certain material has.

Reflect When light bounces back off a surface.

Reflection The image you see when you look in a mirror or very still, clear water.

Source Where something comes from.

Spectrum The range of colours that make up white light.

Survey To make a detailed inspection of something.

Telecommunications Ways of sending information over a long distance, e.g. telegraph, telephone, television, fax or e-mail.

White light All the colours in the spectrum mix together to make white light.

Further information

Websites

Speed of Light:
Find out what light years are and how the speed of light is calculated.
http://csep10.phys.utk.edu/guidry/violence/lightspeed.html

Edison's Miracle of Light:
Learn about currents, lightbulbs and batteries; get a timeline of Edison's life, hear and see historic recordings.
www.pbs.org/wgbh/amex/edison/

Lighting the Way:
Learn about the history of light and its many uses, from a Smithsonian Project.
http://americanhistory.si.edu/lightproject/

Animal Light:
Find out how many animals give off their own light.
www.yahooligans.com/content/ask_earl/2003 0122.html

Einstein Revealed:
Read about his life and learn about some of his more amazing discoveries, such as the theory of relativity. Play games based on the speed of light and time travel.
www.pbs.org/wgbh/nova/einstein/

Places to Visit

UK
The Science Museum
Exhibition Road, South Kensington, London SW7 2DD
www.sciencemuseum.org.uk

Museum of Science and Industry
Liverpool Road, Castlefield, Manchester M3 4FP
www.msim.org.uk

Glasgow Science Centre
50 Pacific Quay, Glasgow G51 1EA Scotland
www.glasgowsciencecentre.org

Techniquest
Stuart Street, Cardiff CF10 5BW Wales
www.techniquest.org

Australia
Scitech Discovery Centre
City West, Sutherland Street, West Perth
www.scitech.org.au

Questacon
The National Science and Technology Centre
King Edward Terrace, Canberra ACT 2600
www.questacon.edu.au

New Zealand
Otago Museum
419 Great King Street, Dunedin, New Zealand
www.otagomuseum.govt.nz

Index